# The Trusted Guardians

*Over 350 years of The*

Written by Debra Price

Illustrated by Zoe Sadler

© Gresham Books 2017
Published by Gresham Books Limited
The Carriage House, Ningwood Manor, Ningwood,
Isle of Wight PO30 4NJ
ISBN 978-0-946095-81-0

Printed in Great Britain

# CONTENTS

# THE BRITISH INSTITUTION SERIES

This book is to help you learn about some of the British Institutions that play an important part in national life.

# WHAT IS THE HOUSEHOLD CAVALRY?

The sentries of the Household Cavalry, mounted on their black horses, have stood guard over the entrance to Whitehall Palace for over 350 years. Whilst no longer used in battle, today's Household Cavalry horses remain at the very heart of many British ceremonies and traditions. They provide an escort for the Monarch at every major state occasion such as Trooping the Colour, state visits from foreign heads of state and the State Opening of Parliament. But the Household Cavalry is not just a ceremonial unit. Throughout its history it has fought in most of the British Army's major campaigns.

The Household Cavalry is made up of two of the oldest and most famous regiments in the British Army, The Life Guards and The Blues and Royals.

After his restoration to the throne of England in 1660, Charles II founded England's first permanent army by creating The Life Guards and the Foot Guards.

The King's mounted bodyguard was made up of the bodyguard of his brother, the Duke of York, and some of Cromwell's former bodyguards forming the Life Guards, the first regiment in the English army. Also part of this early army was the Royal Regiment of Horse Guards, later known as The Royal Horse Guards or 'The Blues'. The Blues were always very close to the Monarch although they did not become part of the Household Cavalry until 1820.

In the early days, the Life Guards protected the King whilst The Blues' main job was to help keep the peace across the South of England.

The Royal Dragoons also became part of the Household Cavalry in 1969. They started as a troop of horse raised in 1661 in Tangier, North Africa. They became 'dragoons' when they returned to England in 1683. A dragoon is the term for highly mobile mounted infantry armed with a musket or 'dragon'. Known as 'The Royals', in 1969 they were joined with The Blues to become *The Blues and Royals*.

# WHO WAS CHARLES II?

Charles II's father, Charles I, was executed at Whitehall in 1649 at the height of the English Civil War. Oliver Cromwell defeated Charles II at the Battle of Worcester in September 1651 and exiled him from England. Although Charles II was proclaimed king by his supporters in 1649, England was governed by Oliver Cromwell until Cromwell's death. It was not until 1660 that the monarchy was restored and Charles II was asked to return to Britain.

## History Detective:

**Imagine you are Charles II.**

1 How do you think Charles II felt when he was asked to return to England as king?

2 Why do you think he founded England's first army? Why might Charles have wanted to create his own bodyguard? Why do you think he founded England's first army?

## See for yourself:

**Visit Whitehall in London and see...**

1 Where Charles I was executed in Whitehall opposite Banqueting House. The clock above the entrance to Horse Guards' archway has a black dot over the number 2, marking the hour that Charles I was executed in 1649.

2 The mounted sentries guarding the entrance to Horse Guards' archway.

# CAVALRY REGIMENTS AT WAR

Cavalry regiments provided an army with soldiers who could attack with great force at high speed, and travel greater distances much more quickly than foot soldiers. This meant they could be used to provide 'high speed' shock attacks, and could also travel about fairly easily to provide information on an enemy's strength and locations.

The impact of a cavalry charge could be terrifying and deadly. Cavalrymen would charge at their enemy using swords to cut down foot-soldiers. If possible, the cavalry avoided attacking the centre of an army where an enemy might try to fire on them with muskets. Instead the cavalry attacked the flanks (or sides) of an army. Here they could pin down an enemy army, making it easier for the infantry and artillery to destroy them.

Sometimes the cavalry would be ordered to charge to provide shock tactics to try to win a battle. Although the use of gun-powder in battles reduced the importance of the cavalry, The Life Guards, The Blues and The Royals still played a very important role in a number of European wars in the 17th and 18th centuries.

A cavalry soldier's main weapon was a straight, single edged sabre.

## The Life Guards' battles:

| 1665 | The Life Guards' first battle was against the Dutch. |
|---|---|
| 1672 | They achieved great success in the Siege of Maastricht. |
| 1685 | All three regiments – The Life Guards, The Blues and The Royals – fought together for the first time at the Battle of Sedgemoor in Somerset. Here they defeated the Duke of Monmouth who was trying to seize the throne of James II. |

## The three regiments played decisive roles in:

| | |
|---|---|
| 1690 | The Battle of the Boyne in Ireland. |
| 1743 | The victory over the French at Dettingen, SW Germany in the War of the Austrian Succession. |
| 1760 | The Blues and The Royals won a great victory over the French in Warburg during The Seven Years' War. The Marquess of Granby led 8,000 men to victory over a French army that was over three times bigger. |
| 1793 | The Blues and The Royals faced near disaster in 1793 when they were part of the allied army sent to oppose the French Revolutionary Army following its invasion of Belgium after the French Revolution. |
| 1809 | The Royals spent five years in Portugal fighting Napoleon's forces. |
| 1811 | The Royals played a major role in helping to win the victory at Fuentes D'Onoro against Napoleon. |

Cavalry comes from *cheval*, French for horse, and right up to the Second World War (1939-1945) cavalry regiments used soldiers on horseback. For hundreds of years the horse has played an important role in battles. From well before Roman times horses have carried soldiers to war. Horses enabled a fighting force to strike at great speed and with maximum impact.

# History Detective:

1  Write your own account of what you think it would have been like to take part in a cavalry charge.

2  Why do you think the increase in the use of gun-powder made the use of cavalry less important in battle?

# See for yourself:

**Visit The Household Cavalry Museum and see...**

1  The uniform of an 18th century Royal Horse Guards officer.

2  A copy of a painting of The Marquess of Granby by Sir Joshua Reynolds. John Manners, Marquess of Granby commanded the British cavalry in Europe during the Seven Years' War. He was a very generous man who cared greatly about the welfare of his solders. Many of the pubs named after him were started with money he gave to his ex-soldiers.

# THE BATTLE OF WATERLOO

The Battle of Waterloo is one of the most important battles in European military history because it marked the final defeat of French military leader the Emperor Napoleon Bonaparte.

The battle took place near Waterloo, Belgium on June 18th 1815 and was fought between two huge forces. On one side were the 72,000 troops of the French Empire led by Napoleon Bonaparte and Marshall Michael Ney, and on the other a 68,000 strong Anglo Allied Army – made up of Austrians, British, Prussians and Russians – who worked together to defeat Napoleon's army. The Anglo-Allied Army was commanded by Arthur Wellesley, Duke of Wellington.

Although Napoleon was in overall charge of the French forces, he put Marshall Ney in charge of the French attack, whilst Napoleon himself stayed behind his army. Many say this was a bad mistake as Marshall Ney had previously made a number of mistakes in battle.

Napoleon planned to strike first and try to defeat the allied forces one by one before they could unite together to attack him. But Napoleon made another bad mistake by waiting until midday to attack because he wanted to let the waterlogged ground dry after the previous night's storm. This delay gave Prussian troops time to march to Waterloo to help Wellington. The arrival of 30,000 Prussian troops was a turning point in the battle. Napoleon's army mounted a strong attack against the British and if the Prussians had not arrived it is likely that Wellington's army would have been defeated.

The Duke of Wellington described The Battle of Waterloo as the 'nearest run thing you ever saw in your life', and British cavalry regiments played an important role. At Quatre Bras, the 1st Life Guards rescued two British cavalry regiments from French lancers and were congratulated by the Earl of Uxbridge, commander of the cavalry: 'Well done the Life Guards, you have saved the honour of the British cavalry.'

During the battle Marshall Ney tried again and again to break the centre of Wellington's army. Wellington knew he had to do something to prevent his army being over-run by the French. So, he ordered the British cavalry brigades to charge at the French infantry to stop their advance. The noise of swords striking armour was like 'the ringing of ten thousand anvils.' After fierce fighting the British cavalry succeeded in protecting the centre of Wellington's army.

The Royals won a special prize; they captured the Eagle of the French 105th Regiment. This was a silver eagle mounted on a flag pole carrying the colours of the French regiment. Loss of a regiment's eagle was very rare, and a great triumph for those who captured it. In commemoration of their triumph an eagle is now worn on the uniform of The Blues and Royals.

It is estimated that the French suffered more than 33,000 casualties at the Battle of Waterloo and the Anglo-Allied army more than 22,000.

# History Detective:

1   Why do you think that Napoleon lost the Battle of Waterloo?

2   Draw your own picture of the events of the Battle of Waterloo.

# See for yourself:

**Visit The Household Cavalry Museum or look on their website www.householdcavalrymuseum.co.uk and see...**

1   The bugle in the Household Cavalry Museum on which the Household Brigade Charge was sounded by 16-year old John Edwards, Major General Lord Somerset's trumpet orderly of the day.

2   A hoof (with a lock of hair) which belonged to Marengo, the horse that Napoleon rode at Waterloo. The hoof has been made into a silver table snuff box.

# TWO MEN WHO MADE HISTORY

## Who was Napoleon Bonaparte?

Napoleon Bonaparte was born in 1769. He was a brilliant soldier and rose rapidly through the ranks of the military during the French Revolution (1789-1799). He seized power in France in 1799 and crowned himself emperor in 1804. He was a very skilled military strategist and won many battles and conquered much of Europe. He was finally defeated in 1812 but returned to try to regain his power in 1815. The Battle of Waterloo is extremely important because it is the battle that finally ended Napoleon's attempt to return to power.

## Who was Arthur Wellesley, 1st Duke of Wellington?

The Duke of Wellington was born in Ireland in 1769. He is most famous for leading the army that defeated Napoleon at the Battle of Waterloo. As a child he did not do well at school, but loved playing the violin. He joined the army and directed a military campaign in 1796 and was knighted when he returned to England in 1805. He became an MP in 1806, but still continued with his military career. He was given the title of Duke of Wellington in 1814 and went on to lead his most famous campaign at the Battle of Waterloo. When he came back to Britain he was treated as a national hero and given a great fortune of £400,000 as his reward. He became Commander in Chief of the army in occupied France until 1818.

In 1828 he became Prime Minister and was known as 'the Iron Duke'. The Duke of Wellington died in 1852 and was buried in St Paul's Cathedral. There are many statues and tributes in Britain honouring the Duke for his great military successes. Perhaps the most famous are The Wellington Arch and the equestrian statue on London's Hyde Park Corner. The Duke is also famous for giving his name to 'Wellington boots'.

# History Detective:

1   Prepare a timeline of the major events in the life of Napoleon Bonaparte.

2   Carry out your own research and explain how Wellington came to give his name to 'Wellington boots'.

3   The Duke of Wellington was most famous as a brilliant military commander, but was he as successful as a Prime Minister? Carry out your research to find out more about what kind of Prime Minister the Duke was.

# See for yourself:

**Explore London and see...**

1   Waterloo Station: In 2015 a memorial remembering soldiers who died in the Battle of Waterloo was unveiled at Waterloo Station, marking the 200th anniversary of the battle. The memorial is a scaled-up replica of the Waterloo campaign medal that was presented to every soldier who fought in the battle.

2   Visit London's Hyde Park Corner and see the famous statue of the Duke of Wellington and the Wellington Memorial Arch. You could also visit Apsley House, the Duke's London home.

3   See the Earl of Uxbridge's artificial leg in the Household Cavalry Museum. Lord Uxbridge commanded the cavalry at Waterloo. Towards the end of the battle, he was sitting on his horse beside the Duke of Wellington when a shot blew away his knee. He is reported to have said to the Duke of Wellington, 'By God, sir, I've lost my leg'. The Duke, who did not like Lord Uxbridge, replied coolly, 'By God, sir, so you have.'

Lord Uxbridge's leg was amputated above the knee and he was fitted with a canvas covered wooden leg which is on display in the Household Cavalry Museum.

# SPECIAL HISTORY INVESTIGATION

### Who captured the eagle?

In the fierce fighting that took place at the Battle of Waterloo on 18th June 1815 **Captain Alexander Kennedy Clark** and **Corporal Francis Styles** both claim to have captured the eagle of the French 105th.

Carry out your own investigation by reading the sources (A) to (G) overleaf and weighing up the evidence provided by different individuals, to decide who you think was responsible for capturing the French eagle.

a) Which sources do you think support Captain Clark's claim to have captured the eagle?

b) Which sources do you think support Corporal Styles?

c) Are there any sources that disagree about key pieces of information?

d) Having read all of the sources write your own account of how you think the eagle of the French 105th was captured.

e) Who do you think deserves the credit for capturing the eagle?

## Source A

**Captain Kennedy Clark wrote to Lord Uxbridge on 10th June 1817, nearly two years after the Battle of Waterloo.**

'When I first saw it (the eagle and colour), it was perhaps about forty yards to my left a little in my front... I gave the order to my squadron, "Right shoulders forward, attack the colour," leading direct on the point myself. On reaching it, I ran my sword into the (French) officer's right side... He was a little to my left side, and he fell to that side with the eagle across my horse's head. I tried to catch it with my left hand, but could only touch the fringe of the flag, and it is probable that it would have fallen to the ground, had it not been prevented by the neck of Corporal Styles' horse, who came up close to my left at the instant, and against which it fell... I called out... "Secure the colour, secure the colour, it belongs to me." On taking up the eagle, I endeavoured to break the eagle from the pole...; but I could not break it. Corporal Styles said, "Pray, sir, do not break it", on which I replied, "Very well, carry it to the rear as fast as you can, it belongs to me."'

## Source B

**In an investigation to decide who captured the French eagle, an investigating officer received accounts from Private Anderson and Private Wilson who both fought in the battle, and wrote this report:**

'Private Anderson was to the left of Captain Clark when he stabbed the (French) officer. He and the officer fell and the eagle fell across the heads of his and Captain Clark's horses and against that of Corporal Styles. Captain Clark called out twice, "Secure the colour". Corporal Styles seized it and carried off the eagle to the rear.'

'Private Wilson was about to quit the field when he heard Captain Clark call out to "Secure the colour" and turned about to assist in taking it. He was a horse's length to the right of Captain Clark when he stabbed the officer who carried it. The colour and the eagle fell against the neck of Corporal Styles's horse who snatched it up and galloped off to the rear.'

## Source C

**Five days after the Battle of Waterloo Colonel Clifton wrote to the Cavalry Commander, Colonel Felton Hervey:**

*'I have particularly to mention my entire satisfaction with the conduct of Brevet-Lieutenant-Colonel Dorville…. As well as Brigade Major Radclyffe and Captain Clark… the latter of whom contributed in a great degree in capturing the eagle.'*

## Source D

**A week after the Battle of Waterloo, Captain Kennedy Clark wrote a letter to his sister:**

*'I had the honour to stab the bearer of the 45th battalion of infantry and take the eagle which is now in London. It is a very handsome blue silk flag with a large gilt eagle on top of the pole with the wings spread.'*

(Can you spot the mistake?  Captain Kennedy Clark took the eagle from the 105th regiment NOT the 45th.)

## Source E

**Captain Kennedy Clark was wounded at Waterloo, and during his recovery wrote to his commanding officer Colonel Dorville about his efforts to capture the eagle:**

*'I give you my solemn word of honour that I do not believe the standard bearer was touched by anyone until I reined up my horse and ran my sword through his right side above the kidneys, when he fell more than half down and I could touch part of the silk cord but could not hold it……. If you think I have no claim, please tell me and I shall be obliged to you for your candour.'*

## Source F

**Major Radcliffe fought at the Battle of Waterloo and wrote a letter about what he saw.  On 7th July 1815 Major Radcliffe wrote from Brussels to General Sir Henry Fane:**

*'(The charge) was a magnificent sight.  … Before I was out of shot, I saw with pride and pleasure Corporal Styles of The Royals bringing away an eagle which he had the good fortune to take….. I have not seen anyone who had the good fortune to remain all the time, and able to give me any clear account of the event which followed.'*

## Source G

**Lieutenant George Gunning, Corporal Styles's former troop commander wrote:**

*'I saw an eagle among a small body (of men). I told Corporal Styles to secure it, and led the men on to the attack. At this moment I saw no officer near me. I killed the French officer who commanded the party, whose sword passed between my arm and my body… It was the work of a moment. I saw the eagle in the hands of Corporal Styles and I ordered him to leave the field…'*

(Sources taken from www.waterloo-campaign.nl/bestanden/files/notes/june18/note.19.pdf - 14th July 2013)

# FROM THE CRIMEA TO THE BOER WAR

The Prince Regent was so impressed by the bravery of the Household Cavalry at Waterloo that he made himself Colonel-in-Chief of the 1st and 2nd Life Guards, and in 1827 promoted The Blues officially to The Household Cavalry.

After the Battle of Waterloo, the Household Cavalry saw no action for 67 years. Instead, the regiments were on royal guard duties in London. They were also involved in helping to control riots. During this long battle-free period a lot of time and money was spent on 'beautifying' the regiments so that they looked impressive whilst guarding or accompanying the monarch. Monarchs like King George IV introduced uniforms that became more and more elaborate and impractical. This made it seem as if the regiments existed just 'for show'.

But in the 1850s the Household Cavalry was once again called into battle.

## The Household Cavalry in battle:

| 1854 | The Household Cavalry was sent off to fight when The Royals were sent to the Crimea to help the Ottoman Empire in its war with the Russians. Perhaps the best known action in this war was the disastrous charge of the Light Brigade at Balaclava. Less well known was the successful charge of the Heavy Brigade in the same battle, in which The Royals helped defeat around 2,000 Russian cavalry in just eight minutes of fighting. |
|---|---|
| 1884 | Three Household Cavalry regiments and The Royals formed the Heavy Camel Regiment when they tried – unsuccessfully – to rescue General Gordon who was trapped in Khartoum in the Sudan. The British formed a square – from which they could defend themselves from all directions with the camels inside. |
| 1899-1902 | In the Boer War a Household Cavalry regiment was sent to South Africa to help relieve the siege of Kimberley. Only one cavalry horse, Freddy, survived. |

May 1660: The English Restoration – Charles II lands on English soil

November 1688: Glorious Revolution begins

December 1697: Wren's St Paul's Cathedral opens

February 1793: Napoleonic Wars Begin

June 1837: Reign of Queen Victoria begins

January 1901: Queen Victoria dies

September 1665: Great Plague of London

August 1642: English Civil War Begins

August 1772: Last traitor hanged, drawn and quartered

June 1815: Battle of Waterloo

October 1854: Charge of the Light Brigade

January 1649: Charles I beheaded

September 1666: Great Fire of London

September 1745: British National Anthem 'God Save The Queen' composed

October 1805: Battle of Trafalgar

1853-1856: Crimean War

1914-1918: First Wo

## Over 350 years of Th

May 1660: Creation of the Life Guards, the first regiment in the English regular army

December 1689: The 'Bill of Rights' established

July 1789: French Revolution and the Storming of the Bastille

August 1834: Britain abolishes slavery

1899-1902: Boer War

# History Detective:

1. How did the Household Cavalry adapt to nearly 70 years of peace after the Battle of Waterloo? What changed?

2. Read Freddy's story on page 29. Why do you think so many cavalry horses died during the Boer War?

3. Read the source below about an officer's experience of the Boer War. Explain in your own words how you think he was feeling.

**An officer who fought in the Boer War wrote:**

*'The hour of march is 2pm, or four, or half past seven, provided that no orders come at nine or at eleven. The baggage will be left behind, or else will lead the advance; we think that luxuries like food are better left to chance. We are informed the enemy are somewhere here or there, but if this should not be the case they're probably elsewhere.'*

http://www.horseandhound.co.uk/archives/great-horses-in-history-freddy-58095

# See for yourself:

**Find the Household Cavalry Museum Collection and see...**

1. A silver inkwell from the 2nd Life Guards depicting the Heavy Camel Regiment in the Sudan.

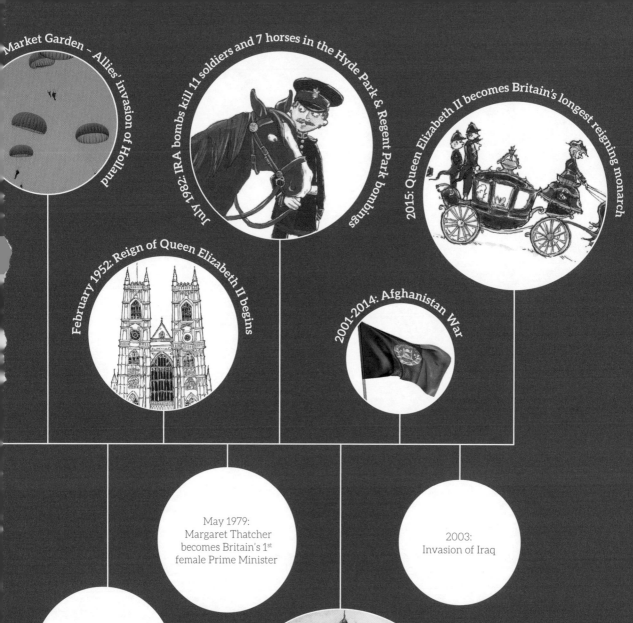

Market Garden – Allies' invasion of Holland

July 1982: IRA bombs kill 11 soldiers and 7 horses in the Hyde Park & Regent Park bombings

2015: Queen Elizabeth II becomes Britain's longest reigning monarch

February 1952: Reign of Queen Elizabeth II begins

2001-2014: Afghanistan War

May 1979:
Margaret Thatcher becomes Britain's 1st female Prime Minister

2003:
Invasion of Iraq

May 1945:
Nazi Germany surrenders – VE (Victory in Europe) Day

1992: The Household Cavalry Regiment is created by joining The Life Guards and The Blues and Royals

Allied Forces land in Normandy

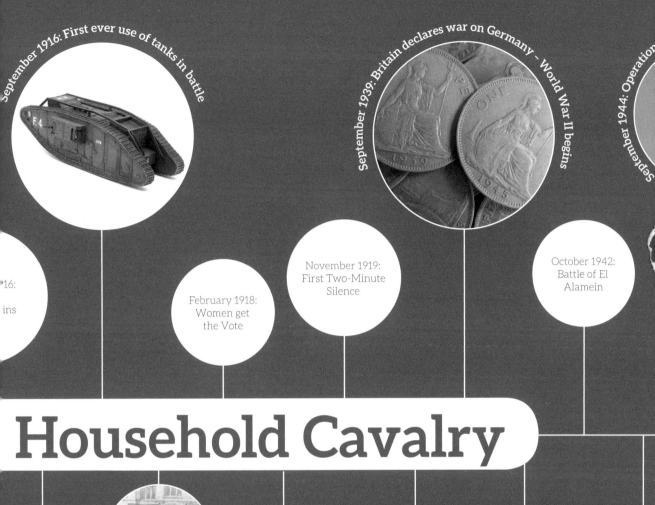

September 1916: First ever use of tanks in battle

September 1939: Britain declares war on Germany – World War II begins

September 1944: Operation

'16:

ins

February 1918: Women get the Vote

November 1919: First Two-Minute Silence

October 1942: Battle of El Alamein

# Household Cavalry

November 1917: Russian Revolution

November 1918: End of the First World War

1939-1945: Second World War

rst day of Battle of the Somme

November 1919: Nancy Astor becomes first woman MP

June/July 1944: D-Day Landings,

# THE FIRST WORLD WAR 1914-1918

**Members of The Household Cavalry fought in the First World War:**

| 1914 | Mounted operations were rare but one took place in 1914 at Ypres with terrible consequences and German attacks inflicted heavy casualties on The Household Cavalry and The Royals. |
|---|---|

*'Shells were bursting all around me, and men and horses were falling right and left.'*
- Corporal Millin.

| 1916 | The Life Guards briefly formed a bicycle company. The Household Cavalry finished the war as machine gun battalions. |
|---|---|

# THE SECOND WORLD WAR 1939-1945

**The Life Guards and The Blues formed two regiments: the 1st Household Cavalry Regiment (1HCR) and the 2nd Household Cavalry Regiment (2HCR):**

| 1940 | The 1st Household Cavalry Regiment went to fight in Palestine with horses. |
|---|---|
| 1941 | The regiment became mechanised and the unit fought with armoured cars instead of horses. |
| 1942 | Fought at the Battle of El Alamein in October 1942. |
| 1944 | The 1st Household Cavalry Regiment fought in Italy. |
| July 1944 | The 2nd Household Cavalry Regiment landed in Normandy and led the advance until September. They fought well ahead of the rest of the allied armies and took several vital river positions from the Germans. |
| Sept. 3rd 1944 | The 2nd Household Cavalry Regiment provided the first British troops into Belgium. |
| 1945 | During the famous airborne Operation Market Garden, members of the 2nd Household Cavalry Regiment led the race to the bridges at Nijmegen and Arnhem in armoured cars. The Regiment finally crossed the Rhine in early 1945. |

# History Detective:

1   In 1914 the Household Cavalry lost many soldiers and horses in the terrible battle of Ypres. Why do you think that horses were not suited to fighting in a battle with guns and shells?

2   How did the Life Guards adapt to the demands of the First World War in 1916?

3   In what ways did the Household Cavalry regiments adapt to fighting in the Second World War?

# See for yourself:

1   The Household Cavalry Museum's videos of the role played by the Household Cavalry in the First and Second World Wars.

# THE QUEEN'S LIFE GUARD

Today, you can see The Queen's Life Guard on duty virtually every day in London. The Queen's Life Guard is made up of soldiers from The Household Cavalry who carry out guard duty at Horse Guards Parade.

The Life Guards, who wear red tunics and white plumed helmets, and The Blues and Royals, with their blue tunics and red plumed helmets, take it in turns on a daily basis to provide the The Queen's Life Guard.

Soldiers are inspected at Hyde Park Barracks and the smartest will be chosen to carry out guard duty on his horse, and the least well turned out will have to be on guard for a longer period of time on foot.

When the monarch is in residence at Buckingham Palace, there is a 'long guard' made up of an officer, a corporal major (who carries the standard), two non-commissioned officers, a trumpeter and ten troopers. When the monarch is away, the guard will be smaller, and is known as a 'short guard'.

Each day the ceremony of Changing The Queen's Life Guard begins at 11am (10am on Sundays) when the Old Guard line up on Horse Guards Parade. The New Guard leaves Hyde Park Barracks at 10.28 on weekdays and at 9.28 on Sundays to ride to Horse Guards for the Guard Change Ceremony.

When there is a long guard, upon the arrival of the New Guard, a trumpeter sounds a royal salute and the officer salutes. The New and Old Guards line up opposite one another. Once everyone is still, the corporal major, senior non-commissioned officer and sentries of the New Guard rein back their horses and leave for the guard room to take over their duty; their duty will last for 24 hours. The Old Guard then returns to its barracks.

The two mounted sentries are called 'box-men' because of their large sentry boxes. Horses are on guard for quite short periods of time so that they can be groomed, watered and fed. These sentries are on duty between 10am to 4pm and change every hour.

Two dismounted sentries are on duty until the gates shut at 8pm. Only members of the Royal Family, or government ministers with an 'ivory pass', are allowed to travel in a vehicle under Horse Guards arch.

Every day at 4pm there is a short inspection in the yard when the duty officer inspects the Guard to make sure that they are well turned out; this is known as the '4 o'clock Inspection' or Dismounting Ceremony. The guards are inspected by an officer and the mounted guards then take the horses back to the stables for the night.

This 4 o'clock Inspection began in 1894 when Queen Victoria discovered the entire guard drinking and gambling while on duty. As a punishment she said that the guard had to be inspected every day at 4pm by an officer for the next 100 years. Although the 100 years' punishment finished in 1994, the reigning Queen Elizabeth II felt that a fine tradition had been established and that the 4 o'clock Inspections should continue.

# History Detective:

1   Write your own account of Queen Victoria discovering the guard drinking and gambling in 1894 and handing out her punishment.

2   Write an account of what you think it would be like to be a soldier on guard duty today.

# See for yourself:

1   The Changing The Queen's Life Guard ceremony takes place every day at London's Horse Guards Parade at 11am on weekdays and 10am on Sundays.

2   The 4 o'clock Inspection takes place every day in the yard at Horse Guards.

# HORSE GUARDS PARADE

Horse Guards Parade is a large parade ground off Whitehall in central London. As well as being the place for changing The Queen's Life Guard, a number of other special events take place here, like Trooping the Colour, which celebrates the Queen's Birthday and Beating Retreat. Beating Retreat is a great spectacle of military music and precision drill carried out by the Mounted Bands of the Household Cavalry and the Massed Bands of the Household Division.

## Daily routine of The Queen's Life Guard

| | |
|---|---|
| 05:30 | Reveille for New Guard in Hyde Park Barracks |
| 06:00 | Stables |
| 06:15 - 06:45 | Guard Exercise – exercising guard horses |
| 07:00 | Gates to Horse Guards open |
| 07:00 | Feed horses and breakfast for the guard |
| 08:00 - 09:00 | Grooming |
| 09:00 - 09:30 | Guard dresses |
| 09:30 - 10:00 | Horses turned out on Regimental Parade Square |
| 10:00 | Inspection, Hyde Park Barracks |
| 10:28 | Queen's Life Guard leaves Hyde Park Barracks |
| 10:50 | Old Guard forms up on Horse Guards Parade |
| 11:00 | New Guard arrives, Guard room handed over |
| 11:25 | Old Guard returns to Hyde Park Barracks |
| 10:00 - 16:00 | Mounted Dutymen change over on the hour |
| 12:00 - 20:00 | Dismounted Sentries change over every two hours |
| 16:00 | Inspection of The Queen's Life Guard – 'the 4 o'clock' |
| 20:00 | Gates to Horse Guards shut |

# THE HOUSEHOLD CAVALRY MOUNTED REGIMENT

The Household Cavalry Mounted Regiment was formed at the end of the Second World War to provide ceremonial duties, with two squadrons of 100 men from The Life Guards and The Blues.

You can see the mounted soldiers on their black horses on every major ceremonial occasion. The Regiment is based in Hyde Park Barracks, which has been the home of the Household Cavalry since 1798. There are 220 horses stabled in the barracks, but as there is so little space the stables are located on two floors, one above the other, in 'double-deckers'. There are another 60 horses stabled at the Household Cavalry's training wing in Windsor.

The Household Cavalry Mounted Regiment carries out a number of special duties which include providing Sovereign's Escorts for major occasions such as:

- Trooping the Colour
- State visits from foreign Heads of State
- State Opening of Parliament

The regiment also takes part in a number of less well known dismounted parades, the largest including the annual service in St George's Chapel in Windsor Castle for the Order of the Garter, when the Regiment lines the route that the Queen and the Companions of the Order take through the Castle.

Soldiers of the Household Cavalry also line the staircases in Buckingham Palace for State Banquets and the staircase in the House of Lords during the State Opening of Parliament.

# History Detective:

1   Draw a picture of one of the events where the Household Cavalry Regiment provides an escort for the Sovereign such as the State Opening of Parliament.

2   A ceremony similar to Trooping the Colour dates back to Tudor times. In 1748, it was decided that this parade would be a very good way to celebrate the official birthday of the Sovereign. Today, this colourful event is still a very important part of the Sovereign's official birthday celebrations in June. Why do you think it is important to continue to celebrate Trooping the Colour today?

# See for yourself:

**Visit London and see...**

1   You can see events like Trooping the Colour for yourself if you visit London, or on television, or online. Look out for the regiments of the Household Cavalry.

# THE HORSES OF THE HOUSEHOLD CAVALRY

The horses of the Household Cavalry are known as Cavalry Blacks. Most of the Cavalry's horses are a cross of Irish Draughts and Thoroughbreds.

A ceremonial horse has to carry about 25kg of kit plus the weight of a soldier.

Cavalry Blacks are usually at least 16.2 hands (1.65 metres) high at the shoulder, and are often bigger.

Most cavalry horses are black, although trumpeters traditionally ride 'greys' – this made them easier to see in a battle.

Drum horses are the largest, Shire or Clydesdale crosses, as they have to carry the great weight of the solid silver ceremonial kettle drums.

Most Cavalry Blacks are bought when they are three or four years old. They are usually named after battles or significant individuals or places. Each year the new horses' names start with the same letter of the alphabet. For example, in 2016, Quiberon, Quasimodo and Quintessence.

Each horse has its own unique regimental number engraved on its hooves.

On average, each horse is trained for about six months before taking part in their first ceremonial event.

Every summer the regiment spend four weeks in Norfolk where the horses get the opportunity to go in the sea. The horses go on holiday 'out to grass' twice a year for a good rest from their duties.

Most Cavalry Blacks retire when they are about 17 or 18 years old, but some carry on until their early 20s.

# History Detective:

1   Draw a picture of a cavalry black or a drum horse.

2   Oral history helps us understand the lives and feelings of others.
    In 2014, Lance Corporal of Horse Horse Wesley Brown described learning to ride:

    *'(it took) 16 weeks training to ride but it felt more like 2 years. It is one of the hardest courses I have ever done. In the riding school arena in Windsor is the most scared I have ever been in the army and I have been on 3 tours of duty in Afghanistan and 2 tours in Iraq (and race fast bikes!). But being on a horse - I didn't like it.'*

    From this account, how hard do you think it is to learn to ride and become a mounted cavalry soldier?

# See for yourself:

1   At every parade you will see a farrier. The farrier carries a highly polished axe. One side of the axe is a giant spike which was used to kill horses that had been badly wounded in battle. The axe was used to chop off the horses' hooves. This came about because, from time to time, some soldiers would earn extra money by selling their very expensive cavalry horse, and then reporting back to the regiment that their horse had died. To stop this from happening, soldiers had to provide evidence of their horse's death by producing its hooves which were branded with the horse's unique regimental number.

# THREE HORSES WHO MADE HISTORY

## Copenhagen

Copenhagen was the Duke of Wellington's great war horse which the Duke most famously rode at the Battle of Waterloo. Compared to today's cavalry horses, Copenhagen was quite small, standing just 15.1 hands. Despite his small stature he had tremendous staying power and carried the Duke for 17 hours at Waterloo.

Copenhagen's career began as a race horse, but he only won two races. His owner, Lord Grosvenor, sold the stallion to General Sir Charles Stewart who was the Duke of Wellington's Adjutant General, and in 1812 General Stewart sold the five-year old Copenhagen to Wellington for around 400 guineas.

The Duke of Wellington had around 15 horses, but Copenhagen is the horse that the Duke chose to ride at Waterloo. Copenhagen had a reputation for being very calm in dangerous situations. At Quatre Bras, the Duke had ridden to the head of his forces to see the enemy. Behind him was a large fence and ditch lined with soldiers from the 92nd Highlanders. Without warning some French dragoons advanced towards the Duke. Realising he would be cornered, the Duke shouted to the Highlanders to lie down so that he could escape by jumping the fence back to safety. Copenhagen soared over the fence, the ditch and the Highlanders!

Copenhagen eventually retired back to Stratfield Saye, the home of the Duke of Wellington, where together he and the Duke enjoyed their hunting. The Duchess of Wellington was so fond of Copenhagen that she wore a bracelet made from his hair.

Copenhagen died at the age of 28, in February 1836. The Duke ordered that Copenhagen's burial should have full military honours with a salute fired over his grave. On Copenhagen's death the Duke said, *'There may have been faster horses, no doubt some handsomer, but for bottom and endurance I never saw his fellow.'*

## Freddy

In 1899 a regiment of the Household Cavalry was sent to fight in the Boer War in South Africa. Freddy was one of around 550 horses that set off for this campaign, but he was the only one to return.

The number of horses lost in the Boer war was horrifying. Many of the horses died on the month long sea voyage to Table Bay. Most died of disease or exhaustion. On their first day in South Africa, at the hottest time of the year, horses found themselves in action with no water and no rest after the difficult sea journey.

Freddy was always ridden by Corporal of Horse Stephens, and from February to August they covered around 1,780 miles. There was never enough to eat, and seldom enough water. Over this period Freddy took part in five major actions and many charges.

Freddy returned home back to Southampton exactly a year after leaving and travelled back to Windsor. The next year he was the lead horse of the Household Cavalry Musical Ride which was performing at the Royal Tournament.

Queen Alexandra asked why Freddy had no campaign medal and insisted that he be awarded one immediately. Freddy was given a medal with five clasps in recognition of his action at Wittenberg, Kimberley, Paarderberg, Driefontein and Transvaal. Thereafter, Freddy wore his medal on his breastplate at every parade.

Freddy retired from duty in 1905 but remained living at Windsor after his retirement until he died of old age, aged 18, and was buried under the regimental parade square.

## Sefton

Sefton is one of the most famous horses of the Household Cavalry. He became famous because he survived a terrorist car bomb attack in Hyde Park.

Sefton was born in Ireland in 1963. He was half Irish Draught and half Thoroughbred. When he was four years old he was bought for around £275 by the Army Purchasing Commission and shipped to England to be trained by the Household Cavalry with around 25 other horses.

He was named Sefton after Lord Sefton, a former Household Cavalry officer, but he was known by soldiers as Sharky because he had a reputation for biting.

He was broken in by Trooper McGregor and this took longer than usual because Sefton knew his own mind and and would not obey the rider's commands. He eventually graduated in June 1968 and his regimental number 5/816 was engraved into one of his hind hooves.

However, it soon became clear that Sefton was a very difficult horse to ride; he fidgeted when he should be still, and worst of all sometimes he 'napped' (this means he refused to leave the stables or turned to return home against his rider's wishes). To try to overcome these problems Sefton was sent with The Blues and Royals to Germany. Here he joined the Weser Vale Hunt, where the hunt chased volunteer runners. This involved horse and rider galloping and jumping a lot of big fences. Sefton loved it! He soon became one of the best and most popular hunt horses.

It was clear that Sefton loved jumping and was very good at it. He competed in show-jumping in Germany and won many classes; he joined the British Army of the Rhine team, and also won a point to point race.

In 1975 he returned to Knightsbridge Barracks and continued to show-jump in England. This time Sefton's career in England with the Household Cavalry was far more successful. He performed his guard duties, and appeared in the Household Cavalry Musical Ride.

On 20 July 1982 Sefton was carrying out his duties and was on his way with 15 others to the Changing the Guard ceremony. Tragically, the IRA terrorist group had planted a nail bomb in a car in Hyde Park which exploded just as The Queen's Life Guard was passing. Four soldiers and seven horses were killed in the explosion. Sefton was hit by 38 metal nails and very badly wounded. His injuries were terrible. He had 34 wounds and a severed jugular vein.

*'Sefton was the worst injured and I knew that we had to get him back if there was to be any chance of saving him.'* Major Noel Carding, Veterinary Officer of the Household Cavalry and one of the first on the scene.

Sefton was taken back to the barracks in a horsebox. Once back he underwent 8 hours of surgery and his veterinary surgeons said that he had a 50/50 chance of surviving. The regiment's veterinary surgeons saved his life.

Sefton and the other surviving horses received thousands of get well cards and and special equine gifts. Donations of over £600,000 were also received and these were used to build a new surgical wing at the Royal Veterinary College which was named the Sefton Surgical Wing.

Eventually Sefton recovered. He returned to his duties. Sefton became a hero, and once recovered helped raise money for the families of those who died, by attending special events all over the UK. He was awarded Horse of the Year, and with Sergeant Michael Pederson, his rider, back in the saddle he received an emotional standing ovation.

In August 1984, when he was 21 years old, Sefton finally retired from the Household Cavalry and moved to a rest home for horses where he lived to the age of 30.

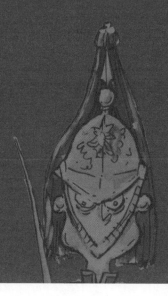

# History Detective:

1 Copenhagen, Freddy and Sefton all showed great courage but in very different ways. Write an account about one of them, explaining why you think they are brave and courageous.

2 There are many paintings of the Duke of Wellington riding Copenhagen. Paint your own picture of the Duke riding Copenhagen at Waterloo.

# See for yourself:

1 You can see a picture of Freddy in the collection of the Household Cavalry Museum.

2 In 2013 a statue of Sefton was unveiled at the Royal Veterinary College, Potters Bar, Herts.

# BANDS AND TRUMPETERS

The two bands of the Household Cavalry play at every ceremonial event, such as The Queen's Birthday Parade or Trooping the Colour. They were first formed in 1660 to play during King Charles II's triumphant entry into London.

At state ceremonial occasions the solders of the bands wear magnificent embroidered gold coats. Theirs is the oldest ceremonial uniform in the army and is only worn in the presence of the Royal Family and the Lord Mayor of London.

Trumpeters used to have very special duties in battle. Trumpeters would play over 80 different trumpet calls so that soldiers would know what to do at all times of day and night.

Trumpet calls included:
- Getting up (reveille)
- Going to bed (last post)
- Post call (arrival of letters)
- Mess call (time to eat)

Trumpeters rode grey horses so that they could be easily seen, and still ride grey horses today on parade.

## History Detective:

1   Explain why you think it was so important to have trumpet calls to communicate with soldiers?

2   Why do you think it was important to be able to see a trumpeter easily?

## See for yourself:

1   Look out for the gold uniforms of the bands of the Household Cavalry at The Queen's Birthday Parade or Trooping the Colour.

2   Can you see the grey horses ridden by trumpeters?

# ON PARADE AND IN COMBAT

## AS WELL AS BEING A COMBATITIVE REGIMENT

Ceremonial duties play a very important of celebrating history and tradition. The soldiers of the The Household Cavalry take part in ceremonial events in London that are watched by millions of visitors to London every year.

'The ceremonial side is really good. I love horses. When you're out in the public and you're wearing the uniform, you feel a sense of pride!

On the operational side not a lot of people see what is going on, but it is the camaraderie that is built behind this that gives you some self worth.'
- Lance Corporal of Horse Clifford O'Farrell.

## THE HOUSEHOLD DIVISION: The Guards Regiments

In 1950 King George VI asked that the Household Cavalry and the Brigade of Guards should together form 'the Household Division'.

The regiments of the Household Cavalry – The Life Guards and The Blues and Royals – formed two of the seven regiments of the Household Division. The other five were Foot Guards and were: the Grenadier, Coldstream, Scots, Irish and Welsh Guards. Like the Household Cavalry, the Footguards regiments have a long and proud history, and are not just ceremonial troops. They combine their special role as the Sovereign's personal troops with their roles in all of the British army's major campaigns.

Over the last fifty years the Guards Regiments have:

- Started the world famous Special Air Service (SAS)
- Provided one of the first battalions of the Parachute Regiment
- Formed entire divisions in the Second World War
- Fought in Aden, Borneo and the Falkland Islands
- Fought against terrorism in Northern Ireland
- Helped to establish peace in Bosnia
- Fought in Iraq and Afghanistan

# Depth Studies:

1   Every day the Household Cavalry plays a very important part in military ceremonies – from Changing the Guard to major parades. Why do you think such ceremonies and events are such an important part of British history and tradition?

2   The soldiers of the Household Cavalry have played an important part in many **turning points in British history** when they have fought to **defend British freedom and democracy** including:

   1815    -    Battle of Waterloo
   1944    -    World War Two: Allied landings at Normandy

   Write about one of these events explaining why you think this turning point was so important to Britain.

3   Copenhagen, Freddy and Sefton are all heroes of The Household Cavalry. What qualities do you think made these three horses be regarded as such heroic figures?

4   The Household Cavalry play an important ceremonial role as the Monarch's trusted guardians, and have also operated and fought on battlefields from Waterloo to Afghanistan. Which side of their role interests you the most? Can you explain why?

5   Over the last 350 years the Household Cavalry has had to adapt to new technology – from fighting on horses to using armoured vehicles in battle, or from using a trumpeter to using the latest radio equipment to communicate on the battle field. Explain how you think new technology has changed the role of the Household Cavalry.

6   The regiments of the Household Cavalry have fought for Britain for over 350 years.  Look at the time line on pages 6 and 7 and write a paragraph about the era of the Household Cavalry's history that interests you most. Can you explain why?